Did the sun shine
before you were born?

SOL and JUDITH GORDON

Illustrated by Vivien Cohen

Did the sun shine before you were born?

SOL and JUDITH GORDON

Illustrated by Vivien Cohen

A Sex Education Primer

AN ODARKAI BOOK
THE THIRD PRESS
JOSEPH OKPAKU PUBLISHING COMPANY, INC.
444 CENTRAL PARK WEST, NEW YORK, N.Y. 10025

First published in 1974 by the Third Press
Second Printing, 1975

ISBN: 0-893-88179-1   Library of Congress Catalog Card Number: 74-82733

Printed in U. S. A.   Designed by Bennie Arrington

ODARKAI BOOKS, named after the mother of the publisher of THE THIRD PRESS, is the Juvenile and Children's book imprint of THE THIRD PRESS.

Did the sun shine
before you were born?

SOL and JUDITH GORDON

Illustrated by Vivien Cohen

Did the sun shine before you were born?
Did the trees have leaves?
Did it rain and were there flowers?

First, I'll tell you how
you became my child
and how families grow.
Maybe then you will know
the answers about the sun,
the trees and the rain.

Not all families are the same. On the following pages you will see some pictures of families.
Which one is most like yours?

Right now, you think of our family as just the people who live with us. Other people who are called relatives are also part of our family. Grandma and Grandpa, uncles, aunts and cousins are all relatives.

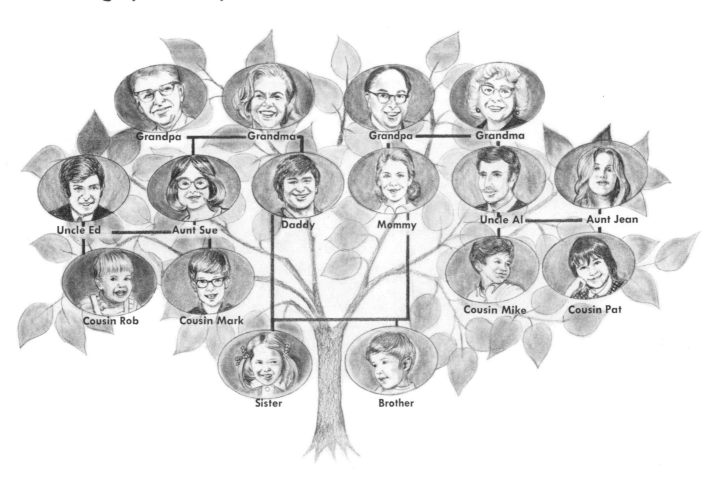

In some homes,
a dog is considered
part of the family.
But a dog is not a relative!

Families grow when new babies are born.

When a woman is going to have a baby, we say she is pregnant.

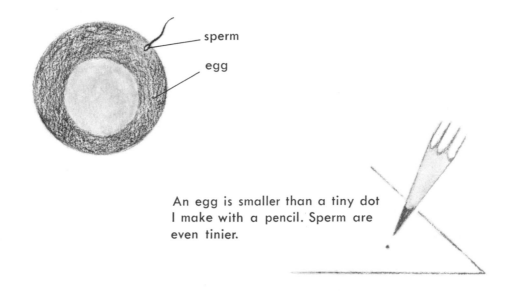

sperm

egg

An egg is smaller than a tiny dot I make with a pencil. Sperm are even tinier.

No child begins all by itself. To start a baby, sperm made inside the man's body must come together with a tiny egg inside the woman's body. Would you like to know how the sperm gets inside the woman's body?

When a woman and a man who love
each other go to bed, they like to hug and kiss.
Sometimes, if they both want to,
the man puts his penis in the woman's vagina
and that feels really good
for both of them. Sperm come out
through the man's penis. If one
tiny sperm meets a tiny egg inside
the woman's body, a baby is started,
and the man and woman
will be the baby's parents.

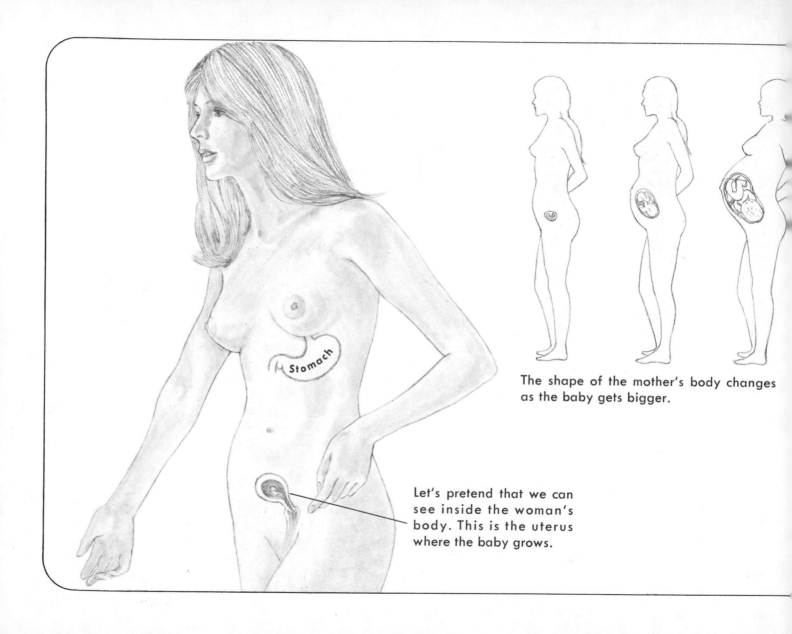

Stomach

The shape of the mother's body changes as the baby gets bigger.

Let's pretend that we can see inside the woman's body. This is the uterus where the baby grows.

The baby grows in a special place
inside the mother.
This place is called the uterus.
It is warm and safe there.
The food the mother eats
helps the baby to grow.

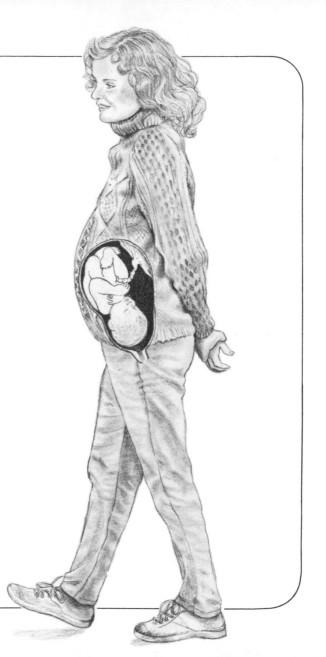

It takes a baby about nine months to grow
large enough and strong enough to be born.
That's almost as long as from your
last birthday to your next birthday.

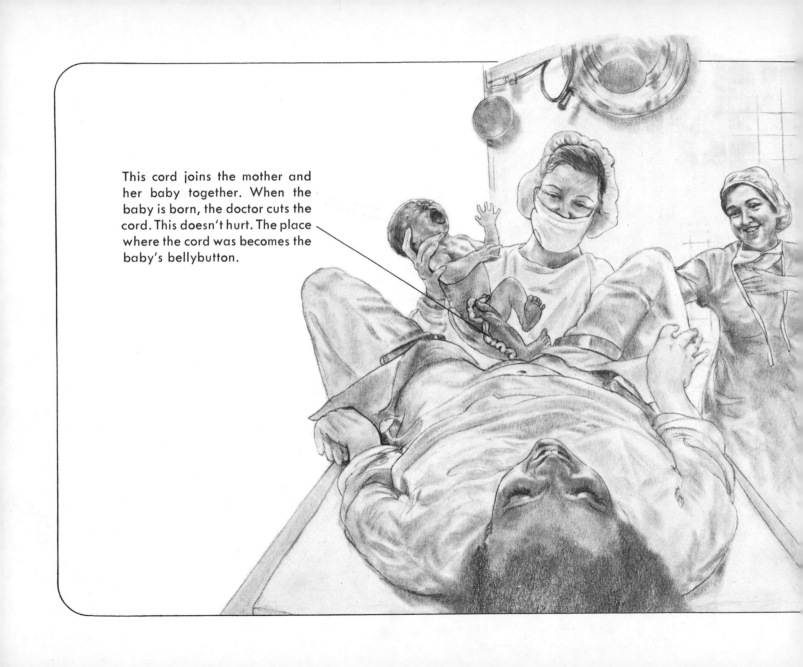

This cord joins the mother and her baby together. When the baby is born, the doctor cuts the cord. This doesn't hurt. The place where the cord was becomes the baby's bellybutton.

Some babies are born at home.
But most women
like to go to the hospital
for the birth of their baby.
When the baby is ready to be born,
it comes out through
the mother's vagina.

There are some questions
that cannot be answered until
the baby is born. One is,
will it be a girl or a boy?
If the baby has a vagina, it's a girl.
If the baby has a penis, it's a boy.

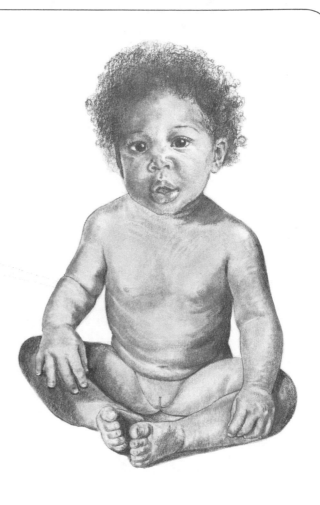

After a few days,
the mother comes home
from the hospital
with her new child.

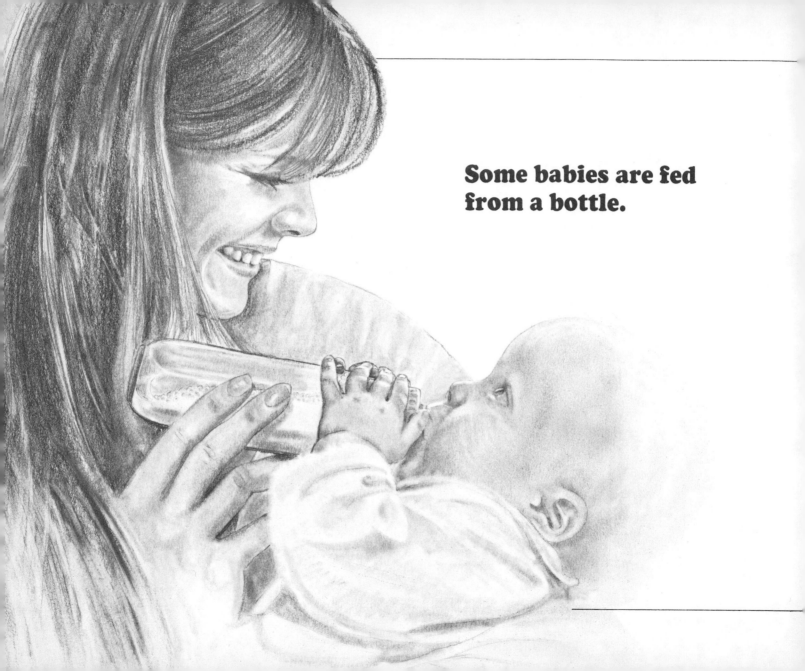

Some babies are fed from a bottle.

**Others drink milk
from the mother's breast.**

When you get older,
many birthdays from now,
you may want to have
your own family.
If you have a child,
Mommy and Daddy will be
its grandma and grandpa.
And maybe someday
your child will ask you
about the sun, the trees
and the rain.

Are you still wondering what was happening before you were born?

There were trees and flowers
and there was rain. I was here.
Sometimes I felt good
and sometimes I felt sad.

Now I am very happy
that you are here
to love and to cuddle.

**Watching you grow and learn
makes me feel good and glad.**

**What about the sun? Oh yes,
it did shine...
even before your mommy
and daddy were born.**